What a Modern Catholic Believes About the **COMMANDMENTS**

by John Deedy

the thomas more press
chicago · illinois

For those also hanging in.

CONTENTS

FOREWORD

First let me say what this book is not. It is not a formal theological dissertation. It tackles theological topics, but not in any attempt to exhaust them or to treat any of them definitively. This book is more an informal reflection, amounting, in substance, to one Catholic's reading of the Ten Commandments. The book is part commentary on the state or standing of individual Commandments; part estimate of what some of the Commandments have come to mean in the theological evolution that has taken place since Vatican Council II. The approach is sometimes personal. Hence, by no means, is this a book that could be a blueprint for official position. Some of the statements may be quite unorthodox. Some of the reflections reach only the most tentative of conclusions.

What I am saying essentially is that this book should be read as something less than a formal guide and orthodox statement. I am not presenting a catechism. I aspire merely to offer a series of thoughts that I trust will be stimulating to some, if not always helpful to all. If I am ambiguous or ambivalent at times, particularly by way of conclusions, it may be because in periods of great transition religion itself can be ambiguous or ambivalent, at least to the searcher. I think it safe to say that Roman Catholicism at the moment is in precisely such a position. Accordingly, I acknowledge beforehand a certain lack of decisiveness on my own part. For this I apologize not. Like so many other Modern Catholics, I am feeling my way anew.

Besides, the Ten Commandments allow considerable latitude for thought and action. Under the Fifth Commandment, for instance, one can evolve a rationale both for and against capital punishment. Though I know where I stand on that moral issue— definitely against capital punishment—I am not sure about some other issues. Therefore more tentativeness.

A small acknowledgment: In comparing the new against the old, modern understanding against the traditional, I used as source for the latter Bishop Louis LaRavoire Morrow's *My Catholic Faith* (Silver Jubilee Edition, My Mission House, Kenosha, Wisconsin, 1961). My reasons are three-fold: *My Catholic Faith* was among the books at home; it is the source to which I revert when looking for simple answers to simple questions—as, when a national publication calls and asks, "What's a venial sin?" (I exaggerate not); finally, *My Catholic Faith* is the *Baltimore Catechism* in spades. It explicates the Commandments as those of us knew them who grew up in the age of certitudes. When I speak of old understandings, mainly they are those of *My Catholic Faith*.

8

Also from that book are the wordings and biblical ascriptions of the individual Commandments. I might easily have found more graceful wordings for the Commandments. I could have gone, for example, to Ronald Knox's translation of the Old Testament for his versions. His is just as handy as Bishop Morrow's book. But what difference? The Commandments are skeletal in expression, and understanding and appreciation of no one of them depend upon the felicity with which it is worded. Besides, from early training we all carry in memory our own wordings for the Commandments. I can read a half-dozen variations for any one Commandment, and each will be quickly displaced by the version drilled into me by the Sisters of Notre Dame de Namur back in the 1930s. Hence, in sum, Bishop Morrow's wordings.

I have likewise settled for Bishop Morrow's coupling of the Sixth and the Ninth Commandments, the Seventh and the Tenth. The couplings make eminent sense. If my reflections occasionally make kindred good sense, I am content.

By way of refreshing memories that may need a little refreshing, the Ten Commandments, or Decalogue, come to us through Moses. They were written, the Scriptures tell us, by the finger of God on two tablets of stone, and received by Moses on Mount Sinai. He made them the basis of what we know as

Mosaic Law. The Commandments are twice recorded in the Pentateuch: In Exodus and in Deuteronomy. They are frequently alluded to by Christ in the New Testament, and summarized in the double precept of charity (love of God and of neighbor) and in the Beatitudes (which may be described as the positive application of the essentially negative Commandments). The Commandments were adopted by Christianity with only one notable variation from the ancient law of Jewish tradition: The change in the day to be kept holy under the Third Commandment from the Jewish Sabbath (Saturday, the last day of the week) to Sunday, the first day of the week.

The Commandments, in precis, sum up the fundamental obligations of religion and morality. It will be noted that the first three Commandments involve man's relationship to God; the other seven, man's relationship with his neighbor. All Ten Commandments are conditioned by love—the first three, love of God directly; the latter seven, the love which, in the ideal order, should flow to family and neighbor through love of God, thereby becoming the basis for justice among peoples.

None of the Commandments, as I have mentioned, is a detailed instruction on what to do and what not to do. Some of the Commandments speak in terms of minimums; some in terms of extremes of conduct. Whichever happens to be the case, the words of the Commandment concerned is never the full letter of the law, religious or moral. The First Commandment, for instance, admonishes us to keep holy the Sabbath, but it does not inform us precisely how this holiness is to be observed. By the same token, the Fifth Commandment forbids a person to kill another person, but it does not permit manners of violence short of killing. A Nazi is not excused because he only maimed a concentration-camp prisoner when he might have killed that prisoner.

All of which is to say that, even without such a thing as post-Conciliar turmoil, the Commandments need frequent interpretation and development in order for their application to be abreast of current morality.

The prerequisite of prerequisites, however, is familiarity with the Commandments. For as the man said, "How can you even begin to keep them if you don't know them?"

J.D.

Chapter One

FIRST COMMANDMENT

I, the Lord, am your God. You shall not have other gods besides me (Ex. 20:2–3).

It was once so simple. We Catholics not only knew who God is, but what he is and where he is. We knew his attributes, his perfections, his all-good, all-knowing, all-present, all-wise, all-holy, all-merciful, all-just, almighty nature. We knew that God eyed us always, watching over us with loving care and keeping a careful memory of every deed and misdeed for our eventual reward in Heaven (most likely via Purgatory) or punishment in Hell. We had, of course, some ungodly problems about the God we knew so well—like that of physical evil. How could an all-kind God permit poverty, holocausts, genocides, wickedness of untoward varieties, chronic sickness and all manner of sufferings, frequently to the most innocent among us? Little children, for instance. Our answers were once pat: the ways of God are strange; God writes straight with crooked lines; God has his own good purposes. Whatever our rationale, God never suffered diminishment. God ever was the

Supreme Being, the infinitely perfect one, who made the world, kept it in its place—and, as Rose Fitzgerald Kennedy wrote with respect to her own travails, never allowed us to be tested beyond our own strength. Under the circumstances, the First Commandment was the easiest of all to accept. God existed; adoration was due him. Though he might be neglected at times, he generally received it. We were aware of the "false gods" of lust and selfishness, and often indulged them. But the True God was in his heaven, and there was no other but he. We endured his mysteries and explained away his vagaries.

There was, most of us now admit, an enormous amount of pretentiousness in all of this. We were so presumptuous about God, many of us, as to shift in his direction the idolatry that the First Commandment warned us against. If nothing else, the modern Catholic is more modest about he who spoke, "I, the Lord, am your God." God exists still, but more as enigma than as a precisely defined entity. For some, not even God's masculine gender is any longer to be supposed. Some among us attack the God-man notion; some speak of "the motherhood of God." (For purposes of convenience, God will be used in the masculine gender in this book. It is impossible to be forever finding a substitute for the personal pronouns "he," "him," "his," and the he/she substitutes are much too awkward.) Some are ambiguous about even using the word God. Leslie Dewart, for instance, has suggested that we cease thinking of God as "being" and devise new ways of talking about God without naming him at all. His counsel catches an echo in some commentary by Eugene Fontinell: "If one insists that the only worthwhile function of creeds, dogmas and sacred scripture is to give knowledge [about God] then I think that the game is over and we are forced from the evidence supplied from historical experience to conclude that they are worthless. But, in my opinion, that is not their function. Rather they must be seen as efforts of the community to articulate its continuing encounter with the 'nameless one.' "

There is much that is unnerving in terms of traditional belief in words such as those. And the unnerving is quickened by Harvey Cox's *The Secular City,* wherein Cox maintains that people should declare a moritorium on the word "God" and wait for a better word to make an appearance, in the meanwhile formulating prayers that did without the word. Catholics can understand, in measure at least, such counsel from Harvey Cox, who accurately or not, has been regarded as an apostle for the secular. Coming from Dewart and Fontinell, however, the notion of the "nameless one" and the contention that we should cease thinking of God as "being" are unsettling. Yet need they be, even for the relatively small numbers of Modern Catholics who can articulate, if only to themselves, the uncertainties and problems to which the Dewarts and the Fontinells give expression? Are not these concerns as old as Christian history? Has there not always been a semantics problem in naming the force which is responsible for the divine order of the universe?

The Modern Catholic may know, or more particularly sense, the theological issues that crowd such quick questions as those relating to God's name and the identification of God as "being," but I do not see many shaken by them—not directly, anyway. These are esoteric issues. The testament of Vita Sackville-West, who was not a religious individual in the orthodox understanding of the term, would form, I think, a logic for many of those Modern Catholics troubling themselves on the score: ". . . confronted with the ultimate enigma, [I] believe, and believe deeply, in some mysterious central originating force which the natural weakness and insufficiency of human nature finds it necessary to symbolize in a name, an amalgam of fear and comfort, which you may call God or Gott or Dieu or Jah or Allah or X, or even 'a pure mathematician,' without any reason *necessarily* to identify that force with our own human conceptions of good and evil. It follows logically that, holding this belief, I share with my fellow-mortals the ancient superstition which no scientific explanation can destroy, but which no scientific explanation has as yet been able to account for: The belief in what we conveniently call the supernatural."

Such reasoning by any appreciable number of today's Catholics is admittedly slippage, large slippage, from the shared belief of just a few years past. On the other hand, most of us are less sure about everything these days. The integrity of institutions, the inheritances of history, the viabilities of ancient givens. Why should many of us be also less sure about God? In point of fact, the concept of God has suffered less slippage by comparison than other primary concepts surrounding our living and being, and remarkably less than might be expected as a result of the death-of-God debate on the one side, and the eschatological obfuscations of certain renewalists on the other. It may even be argued that the two extremes have helped to clarify and direct thought about God. This may be particularly so with respect to the death-of-God contention. It seems fair to say that a decade after the opening of the death-of-God debate—the death-of-God phrase cropped up in theological discussions beginning around 1960 and came more or less formally into vocabularies with Gabriel Vahanian's book *The Death of God* in 1961—God appears less dead than the confidence of the time that people as a whole can get along in the universe without a supreme divinity. How else is one to read the fascinations and gropings of the early 1970s? The Jesus People, the God Squads, the neo-Pentecostalists, the occultists. Quite obviously an awakening of some sort has taken place among a new generation of people. Quite obviously there is a new recognition that human nature is limited and that some greater power exists somewhere. Inevitably this awakening gives rise to a contemplation of God, particularly among young people.

It is very easy to demean this awakening, to spear its shallowness, to cite polls that would appear to indicate that the awakening is much less extensive than surface readings say it is. A recent survey of American college and non-college students, for instance, showed that only 28 percent of the students and 42 percent of the working youths considered religion to be very important. And Dr. William Hamilton of Portland (Oregon) State University, an enduring "God-is-dead" theologian, continues to believe that the word "God" has lost much of its meaning for youths. Many college youths, he has remarked, have never been to Sunday school or to parochial schools and have learned little about the history of doctrines of the church. They approach Western religion "as a strange land," he commented. There may be "fascination" with religion among these young people, but Dr. Hamilton doubts that it goes very deep.

The lack of grounding in religion that Dr. Hamilton speaks of is unquestionably a reality—and a serious problem. But it is not necessarily fatal for religion or for God. If history is forever prelude, as some say, the search for the "ultimate power"—God as God, or God under any other name—will go on. As Dr. Ernest Becker, 1974 Pulitzer Prize winner for his book *The Denial of Death,* has declared, once individuals are genuinely confronted by their finitude, they are on the "brink of oblivion—which is at the same time the brink of infinity." They have then the two Kierkegaardian options: A leap of faith or hopeless anxiety. God will fare well as the choices are made.

What all this translates to, of course, is an entirely new approach to the First Commandment and the affirmations it entails. Specifically, the Modern Catholic—today's and most certainly tomorrow's—will find it more important to sense God than to "know" him (proofs for the existence of God will rank low in the scale of priorities); more important to honor God through the Gospel messages than to worship him through a set of rituals; more important to be concerned about the issues that trouble society than to be knowledgeable about God's attributes or responsive to any mandated principles of worship and respect.

There are dangers in this or kindred attitudes

towards a God. There is, for instance, the danger that social action or some other good work could become a substitute for theology, and belief in God would wither before a pure humanism. There will be such erosion as this, of course. But a God who exists is capable of taking care of his durability, one presumes. He has done so in the hostile atmosphere of officially atheist countries, as cases like Solzhenitsyn's occasionally remind us. He will do so in countries like the United States, even though many good people will lose sight of the supernatural inspiration that at least initially motivates them in their responses to the challenges of their own lives and the society around them.

Michael Harrington has written in *Fragments of the Century* that "the more man created the world in which he lived, the less God was necessary." There is that causal relationship, but the implications are no less threatening today than they were in the Middle Ages, when scientists began unlocking the mysteries of the sun and the stars; nor than they were a century ago when inventions began to revolutionize daily life; nor than they will be tomorrow when feats of our day will pale before new and greater human triumphs.

God will survive. He may enjoy some lesser priorities, but this may not be a negative consequence.

And his First Commandment will survive—

though in constantly revised understanding. It may not always be easy to believe in the words, "I, the Lord, am your God. You shall not have other gods besides me." But God's word in Christ never promised that belief would be instinctive or simple. Indeed, some of us may not always be able to give an affirmative answer to the legitimacy of a First Commandment. But as Father Gregory Baum has stated in not unrelated context, "even when our affirmations fail us, we realize that we are gripped by the inability to believe precisely because we hope for the Kingdom and are unable to reconcile ourselves with so much evil." Substitute—or supplement "evil" with other problems, other temptations, other intrusions on hope, charity and faith itself, and few of us can escape the realization that God is quest and the First Commandment challenge. It is what makes belief an excitement as opposed to a drag. In undertaking the quest, one affirms God, however obliquely. In that affirmation is the acknowledgment of a First Commandment . . . and hope.

Chapter Two

SECOND COMMANDMENT

You shall not take the name of the Lord, your God, in vain (Ex. 20:7).

In the waning months of the Nixon Administration, the public was ostensibly startled to discover that the person who had once made a large issue of the language used by President Truman was in fact given himself to purple prose. Indeed, the transcripts of White House tapes revealed that Richard M. Nixon had smashed all the Truman records. If Truman's language was that of the World War I infantry, Richard Nixon's was that of the World War II Navy, the sports locker room and the pool hall, all rolled into one. Truman's "hells" and "damns" and "s.o.b."s had been superseded by the most exotic Anglo-Saxonisms, sometimes in imaginative combination. And, of course, generous use was made of the name of God and that of the second person of the Trinity.

The revelation jolted a newly sanctimonious public, beginning with church leaders. The Reverend Billy Graham, a frequent officiator at White House Sunday services, rushed out a statement deploring the "moral tone" of the transcripts and, more particularly, the profanity. " 'Thou shalt not take the name of the Lord thy God in vain,' is a commandment which has not been suspended," Dr. Graham declared piously in adding his cupful to the tide of indignation that surged over a self-righteous public, which, one would think, had never used anything stronger than an occasional Walt Disney-type expletive. The reaction was hypocritical by almost any calculation.

In the midst of all this—even, in fact, before Dr. Graham rued the loss of "our moral compass" and advised that it could be found again "in the Ten Commandments"—Father John J. McLaughlin, the Rhode Island Jesuit who served as a Nixon speechwriter, took to the White House lawn and dismissed the profanities that occurred in the transcripts. "They have no moral meaning," he commented; they are merely "a form of emotional drainage . . . a form of release, almost therapy."

The result: Another tidal wave of indignation, this one sweeping up Father McLaughlin's superior, the regional provincial of the Jesuit Fathers of New England, Father Richard T. Cleary. Asked if he agreed with Father McLaughlin's defense of President Nixon's strong language in White House conversations, Father Cleary responded: "I would be standing up against Moses if I did. 'Thou shalt not take the name of the Lord and God in vain.' "

Father Cleary summoned Father McLaughlin home for "prayer" and "reflection."

Now, as anyone can attest who is only slightly familiar with my political ideology, I do not hold any brief for Father John McLaughlin, or Doctor McLaughlin, as he preferred to be called around the White House. Yet in the tempest over President Nixon's profanity, Father McLaughlin stood on solider ground than all his critics. The McLaughlin apologia may have weakened (it became inane, actually) when it got into Watergate morality and the business of the cover-up. But with respect to the profanity, he made sense. There should have been nods rather than further castigations when he remarked to Linda Charlton of the *New York Times:* "I find it very hard to believe that almighty God is going to be wringing his hands in despair" over Mr. Nixon's deleted expletives.

Father McLaughlin did not stop there. There is an emotional release, he added, in the utterance of profanities in certain tense situations. One was tempted to inquire about Father's license to practice psychological medicine, to wonder over the conclusion that a profanity, in certain circumstances, could be a psychological good. But one thought of one's own life experience and let the matter pass.

Now none of this is intended as a defense of profanity *per se*. (Father McLaughlin denied such a defense also.) But it is to say that cultural dictates—manner and good grace, for instance—may sometimes be a better guide in the use of language than some fundamentalist interpretations of the Second Commandment.

Not that the Second Commandment is "inoperative," to borrow from an ex-colleague of Father McLaughlin. It has vast application—although, this Modern Catholic would argue, in senses still not usually accepted.

To return to the language of the White House tapes, an impulsive taking of the Lord's name—an angry "Jesus Christ," for instance—would seem to be markedly less serious, if serious at all, and notably less profane than the *malicious* characterization of someone as a "Wop" or a "Jew-boy" or any of numerous other colorful epithets allegedly used in White House conversations. There was nothing good naturedly ethnic in these epithets; they did not seem to be meaningless typifications. They were bitter and they betrayed underlying attitudes. As such they appeared to be transgressions against charity.

The presumption may not be exactly theological, but it is probable that a God ticking off sins of the tongue in the Great Beyond would be less upset about language that "dishonored" him than language that did hurt to one of his creatures. In other words, the language proscribed by the Second Commandment has no narrow application to God under his various names.

In related areas of morality covered by the Second Commandment, none appears to need more reinforcing at the moment than that involving oaths—the calling on God to witness to the integrity of one's undertaking or the truth of one's word, usually by the swearing upon a Bible or the enunciation of a phrase such as "God is my witness," "So help me God," "As God is my judge," etc. That there has been enormous erosion of respect for oaths was driven home by the Watergate revelations. Many of the nation's most trusted officials lied repeatedly to the public. More specifically, they lied while under oath, thus committing perjury. And they coached co-conspirators in perjury, raising perjury in the process to a kind of perverse art. Understandably, oaths became hollow exercises: Ceremonial actions in one set of circumstances; cynical procedures in others.

That much of this perjury was exposed and its perpetrators fined or sentenced to jail was healthy—not only because wrong-doing deserves to "out," but more positively for the reaffirmation given the sworn word as a value at once civil and scriptural. The unwillingness to overlook the perjury that was committed and the willingness to prosecute was worth a thousand sermons on the importance of truth in the sworn word, before God and country.

An equally sensitive area of Second Commandment morality would concern the taking of vows. A vow is a deliberate promise made to God, by which a person binds himself or herself under penalty of sin to a particular promise, life-style or course of conduct. Vows are particularly common to religious life, and of course they vary in importance according to their nature. As such, vows are different in kind from oaths, and generally of much longer duration. In the priesthood, for instance, the vow of celibacy will be taken for life; in religious orders for women, vows of poverty, chastity and obedience may be temporary, with renewals at three or five year intervals. At the same time, vows may be set aside by dispensation, with varying degrees of ease—or trouble, as the case may be. The dispenser may be pope, bishop, religious superior or other authority figure. Most recently, many persons in vows have taken to dispensing themselves, and herein lies difficulty.

The problems with vows is that they can be trivialized by indiscriminate usage; they can be abused, not only by those who take them, but also by those who impose them; they can outlive their relevance and, with the passage of time, can become of questionable merit/value; they can mean different things at different times and in different places. The vow of poverty, for example, means something quite different today from what it meant just a generation or two ago; it means something quite different in the United States, say, than in India.

The variableness of vows inevitably creates problems with respect to their management and their acceptance—a condition exacerbated by the new spirit of independence felt by so many in the church. This is particularly so of the vow of clerical celibacy, which coincidentally happens to be the vow that authority seems most determined to preserve. It is the mildest of understatements to say that a sizable percentage of the clergy has come to question the meaning and worth of that vow. Whatever, if authority seems arbitrarily determined to the preservation of the vow, and in its most literal context, is the individual whose conscience tells him something different about the vow free to set it aside? Is the individual free to discard the vow if he decides that some altered circumstance, some new awareness of forces at work on him at the time of the vow's taking (parental expectations, social pressures, immaturity, etc.) renders the vow null and void?

There is no easy answer to questions such as these. Each situation is unique, or nearly so, and each involves the individual conscience. Of course, in conflict situations it is the individual conscience that enjoys primacy.

The most that can be said is that decisions to set aside vows should not be taken casually or frivolously; they must be taken in good conscience, and preferably in a spirit of prayerfulness. But when taken, such decisions should be respected, however contrary they might be to tradition or the letter of any particular code. Nothing is more mean-spirited —unChristian—than the attitudes of some churchmen towards men and women who have elected to leave religious vows for a commitment of another sort. Their reactions would lead you to believe that those exiting vows were traitors and moral lepers. These are unconscionable acts of presumption.

At the very least, those departing vows should be credited with an honesty of purpose. At the risk of some presumption of my own, their honesty may often be more genuine than that of their defamers.

Chapter Three

THIRD COMMANDMENT

Remember to keep holy the Sabbath day (Ex. 20:8–9).

Traditional understanding of no one Commandment appears to have been so thoroughly displaced as that of the Third, which directs the observance of a specific day to worship God. For years almost without counting, Sunday—the Catholic Christian Sabbath —was a day on which the individual attended Mass, abstained from servile labors, and, theoretically, performed other good works, such as visiting the sick, attending vespers, spending time with devotional literature. Sunday also was the day when the male head of the house rested and relaxed (not the female head—she continued her daily servile chores, cooking, cleaning and tending children).

Long before Vatican Council II brought its reforms to Catholicism, most of the old ways of Sunday were gone. Changing social mores did away with Sunday Blue Laws (remember when Sunday sports events ended at 6 p.m.?); they routed ancient distinctions between rest and work (remember when a professional writer could write of a Sunday, this being work of the mind and not servile, while a bricklayer could not patch the foundation of his house of a Sunday, this being servile work?); and they vitiated never-on-Sunday concepts about recreation and business (remember when bishops opposed Sunday shopping with a vehemence unmatched again until the birth control controversy?). To changes such as these the Church could, and did, easily adapt. After all, the faithful still flocked to Mass, and they contributed. The institution was as strong financially as when the old Sunday mores obtained—and, to all appearances, was as strong spiritually. Anyway, those old mores were more Protestant than Catholic. Their passing was hardly calamitous.

For Catholicism, the Sabbath crunch came, of course, after Vatican II, when new attitudes began to set into people about what constituted necessary and proper worship of God. Was it attending a Sunday Mass (or Saturday evening, as the case may be) that was short of liturgical and aesthetic fulfillment? Was it responding ever under the threat of mortal/grave sin and being bodily present for an hour or so of a Sunday Mass when you might prefer to be elsewhere? How personally honest and genuinely worshipful was that? Was it responding perfunctorily to impulses that were as much cultural as spiritual, or perhaps even more so? Was it listening to troglo-

gyte sermons when that time could be advanta-
geously applied to some social problem? And why
mandatory Sunday Mass? Were the canons of what
was satisfactory to God to be so neatly specified? If
the Mass is to be an integral element of worship, why
not Mass on a Tuesday or a Wednesday or some
other day of the week? Why not optional Mass?
Why the Mass in preference to some other worship
service or some good work?

Those questions—and many more like them—hit
the Catholic Church in the midst of its traumatic
post-Conciliar adjustment, and the church's leadership was without persuasive answers. The traditional
was to be, world without end, amen.

One impression gleaned by much of the Church's
membership was that regular attendance at Sunday
Mass was of overriding economic importance. Un-
like much of Protestantism, which operates on an
annual pledge basis, the economic welfare of the
Catholic Church is tied to the Sunday envelope and
the Sunday collection basket; under such a system,
regular attendance on Sunday becomes an impera-
tive if institutional solvency is to be maintained.
However much individual Church leaders sought to
minimize the link between attendance and giving,
many Catholics came to the conclusion that giving
was the underlying reason for official insistence on
Sunday Mass attendance. (There was a marvelous

Kieran Quinn cartoon in the *National Catholic Reporter* some time ago of a pastor announcing from the pulpit: "Next Sunday's televised Mass from this church will be blacked out within a hundred mile radius.")

Such cynical thinking is not the only reason why some Catholics have irregularized their worship practices, or dropped them altogether. It is probably not even a basic reason why many have stopped going to Mass. Nor does the phenomenon necessarily indicate a wholesale loss of belief or abandonment of faith, though certainly there must be elements of both loss and abandonment in the development. The point is that no one fully knows what the emptying of the pews means. The slippage in worship as measured by Sunday Mass attendance has been irrefutably documented by Father Andrew M. Greeley and Dr. William C. McCready of the National Opinion Research Center in Chicago— by percentages and according to age groups. The findings are startling, but their meaning remains to be researched and analyzed by the Church's leadership. Follow-through would seem to be urgent if the Third Commandment is to endure among Catholics in some substantive way.

What seems beyond argument is that most Modern Catholics find it easy to rationalize a relaxed attitude towards attendance at Sunday Mass (what the Third Commandment and Sunday observance have devolved to, really), and many have already implemented their rationalizations. At the same time, many Modern Catholics sense what should be uppermost in the leadership's mind: That casualness towards Sunday Mass leads inexorably to another, graver difficulty, one that will become the more pronounced as attitudes become the more casual. The reference is to the matter of religious education.

One of the historic functions of the Sunday Mass has been to provide on-going instruction in the faith: Directly through scripture readings, prayers, sermons, etc.; indirectly by the inevitable assimilation of knowledge and understanding that comes from being part of a worshipping community. It is a function that, however inadequately fulfilled, takes on added urgency with the decline in parochial-school enrollments (by some estimates, Catholic-school registration now covers only 37 percent of the Catholic school-age population) and by the utter failure of the Confraternity of Christian Doctrine or other programs to provide satisfactorily for the religious education of the 63 percent of Catholic young people who are in public or private, non-denominational schools. The worry for Church leadership—and one that is shared by this Modern Catholic, at least—is that if the Sunday Mass vanishes as a point of contact with the substantial majority of the Catholic faithful, lost will be a ready-made means for reaching the people and conveying to them some grasp of faith and the gospel message. The phenomenon could jeopardize the faith as presently known.

Resolution of the problem lies, it appears, in two directions.

First, the Sunday Mass must be revitalized so that Catholics will attend, not out of obligation, but because they sincerely want to, because they find the Mass rewarding and beneficial to their spiritual lives. Special effort must be made in the process to win back the presence of young people, among whom Sunday-observance slippage has been the most pronounced. The Sunday Mass, accordingly, has not only to be made beautiful again, it has to be made relevant. The challenge here is to the liturgical professionals; they must undo the botch made of the Mass after Vatican II. They must know that the day is long past when the Sunday Mass obligation can be effectively mandated. Catholics in increasing numbers will attend Sunday Mass for what the Mass contributes to personal and communal spirituality. If this is minimal, so will attendance be minimal. Further, time is running short. If church leaders do not act soon, they will be talking to empty pews in another generation or so.

Secondly, it seems to me that parents have a special responsibility during this awkward period to keep their children in touch with the Third Commandment and worship obligations. This is not to say that parents should be hard-hat about their children attending Mass Sunday in and Sunday out. An unreasonable firmness will only breed reaction, and is likely to be counterproductive in terms of both individual and institution. However, it is to say that Catholic parents cannot be indifferent, totally indifferent, about the worship practices of their children. By their own example, by suasion, by better understanding the religious instincts of the new generation, parents should seek to keep their children aware of the fact that there is such a thing as the Third Commandment. If it is allowed to become meaningless, then it is more than likely that tomorrow will be the time of general religious carelessness and indifference that the doom-sayers warn about.

Matters are bad enough as they stand now. A recent survey of Washington-area residents showed that 63 percent of Catholics felt that religion is losing its influence on American life, as against 54 percent of Protestants and 56 percent of Jews. The Catholic percentage surprised analysts and, to the extent that the Catholic response reflected personal situations, they inclined to the opinion that the result mirrored "a decline in belief in the potency of the faith." Which brings us back again to the Mass. It is the Mass that is central to Catholic worship. It is through the Mass that faith is fortified and belief renewed—or such is the ideal. In any case, the Third Commandment was made integral to Catholicism through the Mass, and as the Mass floundered, so did observance of the Commandment weaken. The Church ignores this cause-effect relationship to its institutional and numerical peril.

Chapter Four

FOURTH COMMANDMENT

Honor your father and your mother (Ex. 20:12).

In his autobiography, *Act One*, the late playwright-librettist Moss Hart offers the less than serious definition of a family as "a dictatorship ruled over by its sickest member." His point was contrived in order to emphasize the character of the family in which he grew up. His was a family ruled over, not by a sick member, but by a grandfather, "an Everest of Victorian tyranny."

Hart's illusions are, of course, peculiar rather than universal, literary rather than theological. But his citation provides a convenient springboard for discussion of the Fourth Commandment. However overly narrow, the Commandment's conception is in terms of the family; the family is to an extent a dictatorship, whether matriarchial, patriarchial or a combination of the two; and the authority figure(s) are/were to be obeyed, tyrannical or not, at whatever hurt to individual lives.

At least so it used to be. The idolatry of the old catechetical textbooks obtained:

*What are we commanded by the Fourth Command-
ment?*

By the Fourth Commandment we are commanded to
respect and love our parents.

How does one respect and love his parents?

One respects and loves his parents (a) by reverencing
them as holding God's place; (b) by accepting their
corrections willingly; and (c) by excusing and hiding
their faults.

I would imagine that most Catholics, whatever
their degree of modernity, would agree that today
such answers are unreasonable, impractical—to say
the least. Should parental faults always be "excused"
and "hidden"? Is a witch of a parent, or an indifferent parent for that matter, in fact "holding God's
place"? Must parental "corrections" forever be "accepted willingly"; can the rightness of those "corrections" always be presumed?

The answer in each of these instances is an unqualified no. Parental authority indeed derives from
God. But parental authority, like any other type of
authority, has crucial interrelationships. It is respected and honored, spurned or mocked, depend-
ing upon the fairness and wisdom with which it is
exercised. Just as authority cannot be abused or mis-
handled on the institutional level without suffering
diminishment in kind, neither can parental authority
be ill-used without incurring loss. To be effective, so
that the Fourth Commandment can itself be opera-

tive, parental authority must be reasonable, must respect personal freedoms and individual consciences, must be oriented towards genuine sensibilities and rights. Parental authority must also be something less than absolute. It must merit the respect it expects of family members. When parental authority is generous, kind, forbearing and wise, then it is a relatively easy thing to "honor your father and your mother."

The family is in considerable trouble these days, and the causes may be as multiple as the family cases themselves. This much is certain: The situation of which Moss Hart wrote—the situation that the catechetical textbook speaks out of and reinforces—is hardly the typical family situation nowadays. A variety of forces, some cultural, some intangible, has cut into the old tradition by which parental authority was entirely what the parent(s) elected to make it—by which, for instance, a parent could dominate by reason of mere existence. Such social developments as earlier financial independence and expanded mobility enable family members to walk away from impossible home situations that yesterday they would have been locked into. At the same time, quickened senses of freedom and personal rights have made individuals much less timid about resisting family tyrannies.

Much of this has been good for the individual and healthy for family life. On the other hand, it is impossible to escape the conclusion that too often the swing of the pendulum from excessive authority has been to the opposite extreme, to over-tolerance and over-permissiveness, with results of a different but no less unhappy sort. The one common note is loss of respect for an authortiy that should be respected. In other words, I'm not sure that Moss Hart's grandfather of Victorian tyranny was any more deplorable than the parent(s) who, where their children are concerned, don't give a whit what they do, when or why.

Perfect or not, the family is the cornerstone of the society we know, and it is safe to say that the health of that society is measurable in proportion to the general health of the typical family. This family is healthy, in turn, to the extent that it is loving and that its authority figures are deserving of the honor commanded by the Fourth Commandment. The trick, of course, is for the authority figures to strike that happy balance between tyranny and permissiveness—between the iron fist and the turned head. The "honor" that is due is likely to come in direct relation to the success achieved therewith.

One point worth stressing is that the Fourth Commandment is not one-dimensional; if parents have responsibilities that may be oblique, so also do their children. Nor does the Commandment have a cut-off time; the "honoring" of one's parents, for instance, is not something that terminates when a child reaches a certain age or when a child moves out from under the old man's roof. It is an on-going thing that involves responsibilities through old age to the grave itself.

Several years ago as a member of a St. Vincent de Paul unit, I regularly visited inmates of a nearby state insane asylum. This was our unit's special apostolate, and I must say it was not an easy one. I vividly recall the strong exertions of will that I needed to get myself to go week after week. Asylums are not pleasant places, and I invariably came away depressed. It was a relief, almost, to move to another city, many miles distant, and escape the apostolate. From those visits, however, one thing sticks in my memory. It was depressing to visit wards crowded with people who were genuinely sick—but how much moreso to come upon people time and again whose only "sickness" was that they had grown old and whose misfortune it was to have children who chose to commit them rather than care for them in their old age.

Now it may be that there were extenuating circumstances in some of these cases, but I suspect that the extenuation in too many of the cases was the convenience of those who did the committing. It is terribly easy to dispose of burdensome old folks by signing them into an institution, public or private. Yet it would seem that if the Fourth Commandment has any meaning, it includes the continuance of concern for parents after their years are full and they are in decline. To think or act otherwise is surely to dishonor those to whom honor is due. In this context, the old catechism is quite accurate: A grown-up child should provide for his parents in need, and make their lives as comfortable as possible, even when the price involves inconvenience to self.

By reason of involving authority and responsibility in broad, bilateral contexts, the Fourth Commandment, as indicated earlier, has dimensions that go beyond those of family. By way of generalization, the Fourth covers the reciprocal duties and responsibilities of the whole human family: In a word, religious life, civic life, and everyday coexistence with neighbor near and far. Each combination engages unique understandings and applications.

A religious superior, for instance, is due "honor" fully as much as is the public official, the employer, the "boss." In each instance "honor" is merited in relation to how the specific authority is exercised; it does not acrue axiomatically, any more than it comes automatically. Employers, to cite one category, must pay fair and equitable wages; public officials, to cite another, must pursue policies and programs that promote the common good. To the extent that both groups do, they deserve "honor." Religious superiors who practice the counsel of those who define authority as "a gift of the Spirit, which is love," who see authority not as the power to impose decision under obligation of obedience but as the opportunity to lead, encourage and assist in the development of Christian community—these superiors deserve "honor." Neighbors who appreciate that their own well being is not paramount, who live with a sense of humanity and responsibility for other persons— they deserve "honor."

By extension, the Fourth Commandment thus becomes a double-faceted Golden Rule. Honor demands that employers be considerate of and fair with employees—and vice versa; that public officials act wisely and well—with the public in turn responding positively to the effort; that ecclesiastical superiors function with maturity, fairness and understanding—those under their leadership being cooperative in return.

Contempt, unkindness, unjustifiable resistance— these are transgressions of the Fourth Commandment, in the blood family, the religious family, or the human family in its broadest conception. When any or all occur, the best corrective is always love.

Chapter Five

FIFTH COMMANDMENT

You shall not kill (Ex. 20:13).

No Commandment of the Church would seem to be clearer than the Fifth, yet no Commandment points up more dramatically an ambiguity that resides in many Modern Catholics than this one. On principle, Modern Catholics without exception are against the direct, premeditated killing of another person. They are opposed to capital punishment as an extreme and unconscionable exercise of authority. Increasingly they are opposed to war—not merely unpopular, unconstitutional or specifically immoral wars, like the Vietnam war, but wars in general. Many Modern Catholics—though not all by any means—seem actually to be coming around to what amounts to a pacifist position with respect to war, a position stemming in large part from the apparent impossibility of applying traditional prescripts of the just war theory to modern warfare.

Modern weaponry, even weaponry not fitted with nuclear warheads, is so indiscriminate in its effects, so awesome in its power that Modern Catholics in increasing number tend to regard war as a basic immorality and consider arguments attempting to establish a morality for war as an exercise in semantics. An element in their thinking is, of course, the world's vast population. It is just not possible, they hold, to find a place where there could be war and where the civilian population could be protected at the same time—not any more. Yet this is a fundamental condition of the just war theory. Like other conditions of the theory, it has been devastated by technology and by population growth. On the other hand, what if the world were faced with another Hitler? Would the same reservations about war exist as surfaced among so many American Catholics during the Vietnam war? Probably not—although it seems likely that there would be many more Catholic pacifists in any future war than there were during World War II, for which a morality could and still can be argued. It seems likely, too, that were such a war to occur, there would be many fewer so-called "heroic deaths" resulting from unnecessary endangerment of life and limb. Part of war is the protection of one's own skin. Aside from that, however, the reverence that Modern Catholics have for life would induce a keener sensitivity for the prudent safeguarding of their own lifes. Or so I would expect—except martial music and bugle calls do make for reckless heroes. Maybe one had better not rely too strongly on the likelihood of a new prudence, or a different one from the past.

Still this is not the ambiguity which I want to expose. I refer rather to the paradoxical development whereby many Modern Catholics are against war, because of its savaging of human life, but at the same time open to a rationale for another form of death: Abortion—on a limited scale and in a limited set of possibilities. Before the cry of hypocrisy is raised against these Modern Catholics, let it be said that paradoxes and ideological inconsistencies abound in the applications of the Fifth Commandment. Catholic conservatives, for instance, who abhor abortion and condemn it out of hand, are frequently found in support of capital punishment, no less a taking of human life. Also, let one thing be clear: I speak not of abortion on demand. Whatever the positions of some individual Catholics, there seems to be no significant element of Modern Catholic opinion that takes a broad, permissive stand with respect to casual abortion. I speak instead of the possibility of abortion in certain hardship cases, such as rape, incest or a badly damaged fetus. On this medical procedure, Modern Catholics appear to be becoming more open, and not without some theological weight for their position.

Abortion, if the expression may be allowed, makes for strange bed mates. Catholics of the right, for instance, and Catholics of the pacifist left are rarely in the same ideological camp. But they definitely are when it comes to abortion. During the Vietnam war, they were at opposite ends of the spectrum. The right supported the war, standing shoulder to shoulder with authority; the pacifist left, naturally, opposed it by exalting conscience over authority, among other things. On abortion, however, there is no division. Not only are the two groups agreed theologically and ideologically, but by similar routes of logic.

The conjoining of the Catholic right and the pacifist left comes, for the main part, through an absolutizing of the "right to life." The right argues essentially from basic teachings with respect to the creation and the procreative process; pacifists, from attitudes linked to the visible manifestations of life. If these seem to be departure points, it does not prove so. The two are never far apart in arriving at the one conclusion: Life must be respected and protected without qualification—fetal life, that is. Thus, for a religious pacifist like Gordon Zahn, who is anything but a Catholic right-winger, the abortion of a fetus in a womb and the destruction of life in war become one and the same thing. In fact, he describes the destruction of life in war as the equivalent of "post-natal" abortion. "Those of us who oppose war cannot be less concerned about the destruction of human life in the womb," Zahn has written in aligning a relatively small but highly respected intellectual branch of maverick Catholicism alongside Catholic traditionalists and official teaching: That fetal life is real life, and anything done willfully that ends that life is a transgression of the Fifth Commandment.

In between the Catholic right and the pacifist left—or to the left of both, I should say—that body of Catholics is beginning to form who would allow abortion in certain hardship cases. Theirs is a position based partly on uncertainty over the moment when fetal life begins; partly on factors such as the quality of the life to be anticipated. Is abortion to be denied, for instance, in a case where it is known that the fetus will be a hopeless mental and physical defective?

Catholic moralists have long held that life is present at the moment of conception, but now some theologians maintain that that concept requires rethinking because of new biological knowledge. They cite particularly the phenomenon of twinning, or the splitting of the formative cells into two lots to form twins. It is now thought that this occurrence takes place two to three weeks after conception. If it does, the action brings into dispute old theories about life beginning at the moment of conception.

A few years ago, much was being made of the

twinning theory. However, emphases on the mere possibility of life being present, and science's own difficulties in tying together its loose ends, have tended to move discussion away from the question whether the fetus is ensouled or not at the instant of conception, to considerations for life at any stage in its development. From such considerations, some Modern Catholics hold that it is no violation of the Fifth Commandment to perform an abortion in some cases, at least in the earliest stages of pregnancy. They point, to cite one example, to medical theory that many miscarriages involve badly deformed fetuses, and argue therefrom that an early abortion on a known deformed fetus is only to anticipate, and assist, the working of nature. By the same token, some Catholics who have not thrown overboard the just war theory, apply it to abortion, and argue that the "unjust aggressor" principle can be invoked to justify an abortion. For example, they would say, just as a nation is morally justified in acting against or in response to an "unjust aggressor," so in cases of rape and incest might a malformed fetus be acted against, the fetus in such instances being an "unjust aggressor" in the woman's body.

If there is a "liberal" Modern Catholic position on abortion, it is this limited one of restricting abortion to hardship cases. Modern Catholic opinion, on the whole, is strongly opposed to permissive attitudes that would allow abortion to be undertaken at the whim of the individual. As *Commonweal*—which, while reverencing life, has taken an editorial position in favor of hardship-case abortions—has noted: "There are undoubtedly individual Catholics who do not agree with the Church's stand on this matter (and harried Catholic women who will undergo abortions), but we see no evidence of any significant body of 'liberalizing' opinion that would take a passive attitude on abortion on demand, without grave cause."

At the same time, *Commonweal* reflects widespread Modern Catholic opinion when it calls on committed men and women of moderate views, whatever their denomination, to join forces and seek a halt to the rising tide of abortion on demand— indeed, to seek to prevent abortion from becoming little more than simply just another form of birth control, a possibility that may be less inconceivable than was once believed. In this context, the magazine has urged that Catholic leaders abandon their "vain hopes" for any kind of total legal ban on abortion. "In a society as diverse as ours," it editorialized, "such an absolute ban would be impossible, as well as ill-advised," and something that other members of a broad coalition of moral concern would not conscientiously accept. On the other hand, "working together . . . it would be possible for Catholics and others opposed to wholesale abortion to map a prudent course which would permit abortion only for a serious cause, while at the same time supplying full and effective help for women who are willing to have their babies. The legislation that would come from such cooperation would not, it should be emphasized, be all-or-nothing legislation, but it would be worth working for; it would, hopefully, save hundreds of thousands of lives, end the growing identification of the anti-abortion cause with the right wing, and in general call a halt to the national drift toward what many already consider an abortion culture." Many Modern Catholic can say "Amen" to those sentiments.

Less of a problem issue for the Modern Catholic, however newly complicated the issue itself may be, is that of death at the other end of life's cycle—specifically, what the dictionaries identify as euthanasia; what the law—canon and civil—calls mercy killing; and what a new generation of scientists and moral theologians (mostly non-Catholic) felicitizes with the phrase "the freedom to die." Much is appearing at the moment on the subject: magazine articles, pamphlets, and books with such disarming titles as *The Denial of Death* (by Ernest Becker), *Dying and Dignity* (by Melvin J. Krant), *Death by Choice* (by Daniel C. Maguire), *Last Rites* (by Marya Mannes), and many more. The literature is not exotic far-out material by any means—at least not all of it. Some has extremely valuable data, as well as inevitably provocative proposals. If nothing else, the literature points up the fact that with the advances of scientific knowledge, death has lost its medical and moral simplicities. The implications thereof are, of course, enormous.

There is no disputing the contention of books such as those mentioned that there has been a revolutionary shift in death-consciousness, even among Catholics. Yet I doubt that this shift has reached the point where many Catholics are willing to embrace proposals that would make the moment of death a matter for individual decision, however voluntary, or a matter for mutual discussion between patient, doctor and family. Modern Catholics generally, I believe, would reject "voluntary death" proposals that involved direct action, even in the most extreme cases. They would regard such deaths as suicide or homicide, or some interplay of the two, and as a clear violation of the Fifth Commandment. Cardinal Terence Cooke of New York may be no ecclesiastical hero in the eyes of Modern Catholics, but most Modern Catholics would agree with him, I think, in the proposition that there is no "death with dignity" when it means terminating human suffering by the direct induction of death, however voluntary the act.

On the other hand, Modern Catholics are coming

to appreciate more some counsel of another non-hero, Pope Pius XII: That extraordinary methods for the preservation of life are not always necessary, at least not when the suffering is extreme and hopelessly terminal. Modern medicine can keep terminally ill persons biologically alive for indefinitely long periods by the use of medical technology. It is not necessary, from viewpoints of morality and theology, that this be done. It is no violation of the Fifth Commandment to withdraw medicine or medical machinery from the terminally ill, or to use medicines to relieve suffering in serious cases, even when this may result in a shortening of life as an indirect and secondary effect. (Operative here are the conditions of the so-called double effect, where the action placed has two closely related results, one good and the other bad. It is permissible to place the action, provided the action itself is good, is directly productive of a good effect, has a good intention, and the reason is proportionately serious to the seriousness of the indirect bad effect.) Thus, it would also be permissible for a seriously ill person to refuse to follow, or for other responsible persons to refuse to permit, extraordinary medical procedures, even though the refusal might entail shortening of life. All of this is a long way removed from mercy killing and euthanasia.

Beyond this point, the Fifth Commandment simplifies, or relatively so. Murder is wrong, always and under whatever circumstances. Dueling is wrong, although who duels any more? Suicide is wrong, although in most instances suicide is probably more the result of mental aberration than a fully responsible action. Suicides, therefore, are not to be judged harshly, nor their families to be penalized. (Remember when suicide victims were denied Christian burial?)

It is not always remembered, but the Fifth Commandment also pertains to health care, for the simple reason, of course, that health care is related to the preservation of life. The Fifth imposes on an individual the obligation to do nothing that tends to injure and destroy health, for that presumably shortens life. Accordingly, excesses such as gluttony and drunkenness are transgressions of the Fifth—the latter directly so; likewise the former, with perhaps also an indirect dimension. An individual—more especially, a people that overfeeds itself while others slip into disease and death because of lack of enough to eat may easily be in violation of the Fifth Commandment. For the Fifth imposes on people a responsibility not only for their own lives, but the lives of the whole human family. In this context, there are not merely the negative restraints of the Fifth Com-

mandment, but some positive obligations, like promoting whatever would improve the health and lives
of others: food programs for the poor and the needy,
for instance; medical care programs, public and
private; relief assistance of varied kinds. If any Commandment is restricted to its negative meanings,
even though the Commandment itself be negative in
formulation, it ends up with the narrowest of dimensions.

Finally, the Fifth Commandment applies to evil
example and scandalous conduct. These may not
always injure bodies and shorten lives, but the
Church regards them as doing injury to souls, and
holds this injury to be as direct as an injury inflicted
on the body. If one admits the existence of the soul,
there can be no great argument about that thesis.

Chapter Six

SIXTH AND NINTH COMMANDMENTS

You shall not commit adultery (Ex. 20.14).
You shall not covet your neighbor's wife (Ex. 20:17).

At one time it seemed to Roman Catholics that there were no other Commandments so sacred—indeed, no other Commandments, period, but the Sixth and the Ninth. So focused was Catholicism on sexual morality that these appeared almost to be the only Commandments that mattered, the only Commandments of the Decalogue (if two can be conceived as ten). Today, the official Church is still impassioned about the Sixth and the Ninth. But is anyone else half so impassioned? It was remarked recently that the 1960s was the decade of drugs, and the 1970s the decade of sex. It sounds like more than a quip.

The times have taken their toll on the Sixth and Ninth Commandments through a multitude of developments, most of them social. The new freedoms, with their strong sexual overtones, in entertainment, the arts and communications have been a factor. So, too, the feminist movement, with its liberating of inhibitions; certain hedonist evolvements, with em-

57

phases on enjoyment, personal satisfaction and sexual performance; new views as to what constitutes acceptable sexual behavior—thus, new behavioral freedoms. Not all the changes have been bad, by any means. The question is: Has change gone too far? The impulse of the Modern Catholic is to answer, "Certainly not." But then I recall how I squirm when I attend a motion picture these days with one of my children—how I even squirm when some commercials are shown on television, so shot through are many of them with double entendre and sexual symbolism. Much of this makes me wonder if there might have been some happier medium between what was, what is, and what is becoming. It seems on occasion as if we are being swept from new understandings, new appreciations, into outright permissiveness, carte blanche tolerances. The old ways of sexual morality were repressive and deplorable. But as one believes that reserve is worth honoring and that privacy has its place, I now sometimes suspect that the old ways may not have been so altogether bad as I once thought. It seems time, for instance, for reassessment of "now" behavioral patterns where adultery is seriously offered in liberated circles, including some Catholic ones, as a fortifier of marriages and where one is thought square if he covets not his neighbor's wife (or vice verse in the case of females—or Lord knows what in the case of bisexuals). I confess my reservations about the so-called New Morality, but unless I miss my guess (and unless the Sixth and Ninth Commandments have been abrogated), so do most Modern Catholics.

How did it all happen? So far as Catholicism is concerned, it may be argued that authority is partially responsible for the erosion of respect for the Sixth and Ninth Commandments. Authority's one-dimensionalisms on sexual morality—for instance, its determination to hold fast on lost issues like birth control in the face of strong moral and theological argument for reconceptualization of thought and teaching—have resulted in numerous instances of Catholics' taking aspects of sexual morality into their own hands (so to speak) and working out their own moral codes. Yet, vulnerable as authority may be to criticism, it cannot be blamed entirely. For it also has been the victim of societal forces beyond its control or shaping. Let's look at some of these.

Situation ethics, for instance. Who would have guessed when they were reading Graham Greene's "theological" novels back in the late 1940s and early 1950s that the situation ethics that added fascination to his plots (remember the Whiskey Priest? Scobie? Sarah Miles?) would ensnare vast segments of society? The theses that sin brings the person closer to God, that the sinner is the person of true humility and charity were not uniquely Greene's. Similar themes could be glimpsed in the writings of Gertrud von le Fort, Francois Mauriac and other writers, Catholic and otherwise. In any case, situation ethics are no longer the preserve of the novelists. Theologians, professional and amateur, have moved into the territory.

Who would have guessed also that Hugh Hefner's 1950s *Playboy* philosophy of promiscuity—his proposition that sex is just plain "fun"—would take a grip on a whole generation of young adults, and that much of this generation and the one following would graduate to Hefner's world, where anything sexual is permissible (at the least) so long as nobody gets hurt—and if then, so what?

At the same time, who would have thought that "sin" would have lost much of its meaning by the 1970s, so that theologians would be debating not only the esoteric question of whether it was possible for children under seven to commit "mortal sin," (the modern variation of how many angels could dance on the head of a pin), but also whether in large areas of sexual morality there was such a thing as serious sin? Was not serious sin, rather than the violation of some outmoded behavioral code really a lack of love? And if so, does not a literal application of that notion open up imaginative justifications for hitherto proscribed sexual conduct?

Whatever, these and related developments lead

inevitably to the question of whether there is any longer such a thing as valid absolutes so far as the Sixth and Ninth Commandments are concerned. The situation-ethics people would, of course, say no—explaining that principles may be subordinated to circumstances, the general to the particular; that the "natural," the biblical and the theoretical may give way, when circumstances dictate, to the personal and the actual. Accordingly, by way of example, might a situation ethicist hold that unmarried love is not just permissible, but in many cases may be infinitely more moral than married "unlove." Thus are the moral implications of adultery and pre-martial sex discounted. Most situation ethicists maintain that, like any other human acts, adultery and pre-marital sex must be subject to human responsibility and that there should be an awareness of the social implications of the acts. But frequently there is no further dimension of a meaningful kind. On the whole, adultery and pre-marital sex tend to present about as much moral dilemma for the casual situation ethicist as the decision whether or not to watch a particular television show: Is it convenient? do you/ we want to? will it be personally/interpersonally satisfying? is anybody being hurt? The formulation might be tendentious, but in substance adultery and pre-marital sex are involvements that for the situationalists are ungoverned by absolutes.

Can the Modern Catholic live by such a philosophy? Not entirely, if he believes in the validity of the idea that absolutes do and should exist. The Modern Catholic concedes that in the New Morality there is much that is commendable, notably the emphases on personhood and individuality, so often neglected in traditional morality. Still, for most Modern Catholics absolutes have their priorities—not the rigid absolutes they once lived with, but absolutes that say "there are rules," "there is such a thing as a norm," "Life is not merely a behavioralist experience." Where sexual morality is concerned, these would be the absolutes that honored chastity, integrity, sincerity, purity—within a context of love and respect. Absolutes can be annoying. Sometimes they may be impossible. But always they speak a message worth being reminded of: There is the total human situation, and it has a precedence over the fragmented, momentary situation, in behavioral preferences as in any other area of human activity. In the instance of married persons, there is, additionally, the commitment to live in love and honor. Adultery defeats both.

None of this talk about absolutes is to say that the Modern Catholic is wed, so to say, to the letter of out-of-date rule books. Theology evolves. So do understandings. Insofar as sexual morality is concerned, there is considerable room within Catholicism for a reconceptualization of principles. It seems unreasonable, for instance, to attach Hell's fire to occasional sexual encounters, as was once the custom. Promiscuity is one thing, and only the most exotic condone it. But promiscuity is not the occasional sexual experience, the "happening." To regard the latter as fraught with moral gravity is to make sexual morality laughable.

Similarly, a non-judgmental attitude should be adopted with respect to homosexual conduct. Too many theological ambiguities exist, to say nothing of the scientific and biological ones, for anyone to strike rigid poses of righteousness and offended sensibilities. Historically, these ambiguities have been ignored (and in the ignoring, prejudices have been fostered). But at last they are beginning to be addressed, however timidly, by a few Church groups, including the United States Bishops' Committee on Pastoral Research and Practices, which during 1973 offered guidelines to priest-confessors in dealing with homosexuals. Inadequate though the guidelines may be, they are at least recognition that a theological deficiency exists in the face of a human need.

Questions relating to homosexual conduct are complex and multiple, but the fact that the questions are at last being confronted, with whatever reluctance, lends hope that one day an acceptable theology of homosexuality will evolve. In the meantime, though it may be difficult to sanction the alternative forms of sexual expression preferred by the homosexual, male and female, a recognition of personal and civil rights in job employment, housing, public accommodations and other prerogatives which all people should have just by reason of being born.

Traditionally, one of the strongest proscriptions of the Sixth Commandment—for Catholics—related to birth control. The why was simple enough. In the old Catholic moral understanding, the primary purpose of marriage was the begetting and rearing of children, and any attempt to frustrate that purpose by artificial or "unnatural" means was considered a "grievous sin," a violation of "natural and divine law," a sin against the Sixth.

There is no longer much talk in the Catholic community about primary ends and secondary ends, the moreso since Vatican Council II's Constitution on the Church in the Modern World avoided the distinction in its section dealing with marriage and the family. Nor is there any longer much troubling over means. The Modern Catholic accepts the Council's emphases on responsible parenthood and, to the extent that a justification may be required within the individual conscience, the Modern Catholic may seize on the indecision of theologians about marriage morality and thus bypass the strictures of *Humanae Vitae*, Pope Paul VI's encyclical holding the line on birth control. But modern minds are long since made up. The Modern Catholic, male and female, is devoid of upsetting qualms over birth control and not hung up over means that some in the Church might label "blameworthy"—excepting, of course, abortion, which the Modern Catholic rejects as an acceptable method of birth control, even though, as mentioned in the previous chapter, a rationale for abortion under certain exceptional circumstances may be maintained.

In effect, the Modern Catholic rejects the ancient Catholic notion that to "mutilate" (what a loaded word!) the conjugal act is to offend God and to destroy the sign and reality of a married couple's loving unity. The Modern Catholic concedes that an open-endedness in the conjugal act is generally (though not necessarily) a good. However, the Modern Catholic is doubtful that open-endedness (in other words, the "integrity" of the conjugal act) is of higher value than other personalist and social considerations: The fuller development of the individuals involved, or their family, or the wider common good. To word it another way, the Modern Catholic feels it more important that love and unity and the common good be furthered than that the so-called integrity of a mere physical, sometimes biological, act be maintained at whatever cost. This is not so arbitrary a logic as might at first be thought. The Constitution on the Church in the Modern World urges that considerations about parenthood take into account the welfare and social needs of the family group, of temporal society, and of the Church itself. It does not take a long stretch of the mind to move to the conclusion that an assured method, though it may involve artificial means, might indeed be more responsible in the cases of many couples than the officially condoned, highly unreliable rhythm method.

A further element in the reasoning of the Modern Catholic on birth control is the population question as a whole. In the year 1 A.D., it is commonly figured that the population of the world was between 200 and 300 million. By the year 1650, the population was estimated at a little over 500 million. By 1850, it was one billion. Thus it took eighteen-and-one-half centuries for the population to reach the billion mark. The next billion people, however, was only 80 years away; this year (1975), the population will reach four billion; by the year 2000, projections have the world population reaching at least five-and-one-half billion and possibly going as high as seven billion. Young Modern Catholics realize that they are population multipliers. They sense that the globe can support only so many people indefinitely. And they hear Catholic thinkers increasingly calling upon the Church's leadership to confront the population situation, admit its gravity, and drop opposition to the idea of responsible population control. Young Modern Catholics are not unaffected, nor should they be, when they note people like Father Arthur McCormick, M.H.M., writing in *St. Anthony Messenger* that "population control has to be one part of any long-range solution to the inhuman conditions in which many live," and adding that "if we Christians care about the world, we must face up to the population crisis and join others who are doing something about it." Their inevitable conclusion: Prohibitions must be dropped (or ignored) to non-mutilating artificial means of birth control, if responsible parenthood is to be more than mere preachment and be truly realizable.

Father McCormick expressed his concern in terms of the Third World of developing nations. Young Modern Catholics add the dimension of their own milieu. They are aware of the world situation; they read constantly of the strains being placed on non-renewable resources; they see their own country crowding up—and they calculate their responsibilities accordingly. They practice birth control responsibly, and without undue preoccupation about means, artificial or otherwise.

If practice precedes policy in this instance as in some many others of history, the sanctioned birth-control policy of the Church's tomorrow is the now of the Modern Catholic.

One important area of Sixth and Ninth Commandment morality in which reconceptualization is both necessary and possible would seem to be that of divorce and remarriage.

No where has the marriage-ceremony phrase, "until death do you part," had a more literal meaning than in the Catholic Church. From its earliest days, the Catholic Church has held that a lawful, consummated marriage between a baptized man and a baptized woman is for life, and that even where a civil divorce might occur, the original marriage bond persists. Catholic Church policy has permitted civil divorce, of course, for Catholics. But generally only as a legal convenience. Historically, there has been no way that a Catholic who was in a valid first marriage could remarry with the Church's official blessing. Those who did remarry, civilly or in another church, incurred specific ecclesiastical penalties, including exclusion from the sacraments and sometimes also denial of a Christian burial. Apart from granting rare annulments, where either or both parties to a marriage could prove physical or psychic impotency, coercion or some other factor nullifying validity of the ceremony, the Church's position has been an uncompromising one, one which has worked spiritual distress and emotional hardship on countless numbers of Catholics. The Catholic divorce rate is not substantially different from that of the national average: 455 divorces for every 1,000 new marriages. Given U.S. Catholic population figures (48,565,438 in 1974) and the average number of Catholic marriages (over 400,000), some estimate that as many as 5 million American Catholics are divorced and in so-called invalid second marriages.

In recent years, pastors, theologians and lay people alike have begun to concern themselves about the charity and justice of the Church's old positions and, concomitantly, about the religious rights of Catholics who do divorce and remarry, thus putting their consciences and their lives at variance with vocational norms that exist within the Official Church. One result is the budding of a theology that could accommodate divorce and remarriage under certain circumstances. Most Modern Catholics welcome the development.

The roots of the theology are in propositions like that of Father Germain LaSage, a canon law expert at Ottawa's St. Paul's University, who advances the theory that Catholic couples deprived of what he calls a broadly defined "partnership of life" could be free to enter a new marriage; like that of Father Charles Curran of the Catholic University of America, who argues that pastoral practice should be allowed to evolve with respect to remarriage, as it has in such areas as usury, religious liberty, masturbation and mixed marriages; and like that of Monsignor Stephen J. Kelleher, former presiding judge of the New York Archdiocesan Marriage Tribunal, who maintains that Catholics themselves should decide in their own consciences whether or not they are free before God to enter a second marriage.

There is ample evidence that many Modern Catholics are doing precisely that—and with the blessing of many priests. It is, in fact, becoming commonplace for priests of evolved theology to perform weddings for second-marriage Catholics. The weddings may have to be conducted outside regular Church channels, and they may not be entered in official parish registers, but neither celebrants nor celebrees consider the new marriages less valid on that account.

The basic factor at work in this evolution of theological thought is a new understanding of what constitutes an end to Christian marriage. A strong school of thought is building upon the proposition that a marriage that is without marital affection, that is emotionally and psychologically dead, is dead in fact. There is likewise a new interpretation of what the words, "until death do you part," might mean. Might they not mean, "until the death *of love* do you part"? Say yes, and it is easy to postulate the validity of divorce and remarriage.

This sort of thinking is too radical for most of today's bishops, although some of them have become openly concerned about their pastoral responsibilities in the light of the burgeoning number of divorced and remarried Catholics. The chief evidence of this concern is in programs whereby "good conscience" Catholics of stable second marriages—those able to justify within their own consciences personal situations contrary to the Church's traditional discipline—can receive the Eucharist and thus participate in the sacramental life of the Church, a privilege extended without any official decision being made on the validity or invalidity of the previous marriage. The Archdiocese of Portland, Oregon, has quietly processed hundreds of "good-conscience cases" and readmitted the individuals to the sacraments. So has the Diocese of Boise, Idaho, the Diocese of Baton Rouge, Louisiana, and a number of others.

Two years ago, Cardinal John Krol of Philadelphia moved to terminate "good conscience" programs, on the grounds that the Holy See was studying the issue and it was inappropriate to anticipate the Holy See's conclusions. There were loud groans all around. However, the evidence is that the programs, or something akin to them, are going ahead, without fanfare or publicity. The future thus seems predictable: If the practice of permitting divorced and remarried Catholics to share in the Church's sacramental life becomes widespread, it will be only a matter of time before divorced Catholics in ever increasing numbers conclude that it is all right to enter a second marriage. Again, practice follows new theory. More than that; as Father Curran comments, "Once you admit that divorced and remarried people can be reconciled to the Church, you have to admit that divorced Catholics can remarry in the first place." To Modern Catholics, the logic is irrefutable.

The Sixth and the Ninth Commandments have been addressed to this point much as though the two were interchangeable. In the sense that both deal with sexual morality, they are indeed interchangeable. Yet there is an essential division between the two. It comes in the fact that, while the Sixth deals basically with conduct or behavior (the emphasis of most of this chapter), the Ninth focuses on thoughts and desires. The Evangelist Matthew sums up the Ninth Commandment in 5:27-28: "But I say to you that anyone who even looks with lust at a woman has already committed adultery with her in his heart." I suppose the meaning can be extended to the other half of the human race by reversing the pronouns.

What can one say about Matthew except that he puts a heavy admonition on us all. Living as we do in a sex-oriented society, where everything from automobiles to toothpaste is pitched, one way or another, to sexual thought and desire (note sometime how a certain deodorant is packaged), it is virtually impossible to go through any hour of the day without the sensuous in us being assaulted. To exist in America is to live a life of temptation. Catholics are cautioned by their Church against entertaining temptations, but one would almost have to move to a desert island (or, maybe, Philadelphia?) to escape the constant temptations of the nowadays. (Does one entertain temptation by watching that suggestive shaving-cream commercial a second, third, fourth time?)

Many Catholics worked themselves into some severe hang-ups over what constituted the entertaining of temptations—or so one would presume from reading many recent memoirs of what it meant to grow up Catholic. Much of the reminiscing is undoubtedly exaggerated, but the fact that there is any reminiscing at all on such silly details as the wearing or not wearing of patent-leather shoes, for instance, indicates that a consciousness existed about the avoiding of temptation. Today's generations seem much less preoccupied with the point, and this may be as healthy spiritually as it certainly is psychologically. There is such a leap from thought and desire to action itself, that it seems inane to get strung out over the non-concrete.

All of which is to say, I guess, that to this Modern Catholic the Ninth Commandment seems to be an invitation to scrupulousity—so much so that it appears as important to speak cautions about the Commandment as it is to remind about its traditional proscriptions: "Beware unchaste thoughts;" "beware indecent literature;" "beware pornographic films and plays;" "beware evil companions;" "beware immodesty in dress and actions."

The problem about the proscriptions of the Ninth is how to decide what are unchaste thoughts, what is indecent literature, what is a pornographic film, etc. The courts cannot define them. Confessors frequently are more hindrance than help, at least those I have known. Maybe the reason is that as individuals we all have different tolerance levels; maybe the reason is that tomorrow's experience is going to be quite different from today's, as today's was from yesterday's. One cannot even look to self as reliable guide; or, at least, consistent guide.

The wisest counsel apropos the Ninth Commandment may be to relax, not get up tight, not take Matthew too literally.

I hesitate to end this section on a light note. But at the risk of undercutting some earlier serious thoughts, I cite some questions and answers from Joel Wells' "A Catechism of Sex," which appeared in his book *Second Collection* (Thomas More Press,

74

1973). Wells' treatment is characteristically whimsical, but the wisdom, so far as the Ninth Commandment is concerned, is subtle and profound. Let me quote, then duck off to another Commandment:

Q. What of dirty thoughts?
A. Impure of unchaste thoughts are always mortally sinful when they are not resisted. The fact that they occur to you is not of itself sinful since we are the victims of original sin. But they must under no circumstances be entertained.
Q. How do you know when you've entertained them rather than resisted them?
A. There's no way to be sure.

Chapter Seven

SEVENTH AND TENTH COMMANDMENTS

You shall not steal (Ex. 20:15).
You shall not covet your neighbor's house (Ex. 20:17).

Though on the surface each seems distinct enough, the Seventh and the Tenth are two more Commandments where morality overlaps.

The Seventh forbids the taking of what belongs to another, presuming, of course, that the possessor has a right to withhold from the taker and presuming too that the possessor reasonably maintains that right. But all within reason. A starving person faced with the prospect of death would certainly have the right to take food from one with plenty without violating personal or communitarian morality. By the same token would it be unreasonable for one with plenty to deny food to the hungry; to maintain possession at the exepnse of anyone starving would be to make operative a reverse application of the Seventh, the possessor thus becoming answerable in conscience and before God for the act of denial.

The Tenth, at the same time, proscribes against avarice—and coveting, in the verb of the Commandment. In its obvious sense, covetousness is concerned with riches in themselves, whether of money, or property, or fame, or reputation. At issue, in a word, is an unreasonable desire, an unholy passion, for what one does not possess; it is desire which, when willfully indulged and implemented, becomes anti-social and sinister, as inclination gives way to deed. The Tenth is concerned primarily with objects and human relations of a non-sexual kind (the latter being covered by the Sixth and Ninth Commandments). The covetousness of which it speaks is considered a capital sin—because, as St. Paul declared in Timothy VI, it is *radix omnium peccatorum:* "For covetousness is the root of all evils, and some in their eagerness to get rich have strayed from the faith and have involved themselves in many troubles." Add to "rich" and its pecuniary variants, inordinate pursuit of fame, ambition, pleasures, power, etc., and the scope of the Tenth Commandment comes into focus.

Sweeping aspects of conduct and behavior, private and public, are covered by the Seventh and Tenth Commandments. The Seventh, for instance, extends beyond stealing and theft to robbery, embezzlement, usury, violation of business contracts, cheating in purchases and in sales, falsification of weights and measures, deception in any mutual exchange of goods, and diverse other forms of duplicity, such as corporate exploitation of peoples and regions. The Tenth has its extensions in the corruption which avariciousness and covetousness work on human values generally, and which when uncontrolled devastate such virtues as justice and charity. Politicians are easy whipping-boys, and one probably should not use negatively a body so impoverished for talent. Still it cannot be denied that one commonly sees abuses of the Tenth Commandment among political figures, as public official after public official is caught going to the extremes of avarice and covetousness in the acquisition of money or favor, or both, by dishonest or extra-legal means. In such instances, the individual conscience is done damage. But the harm extends beyond—to the common good of the community, which the public official is, in fact, supposed to be safeguarding and promoting. The "perpetrator," in current police jargon, thus is guilty not only of personal sin, but also of a violation of the commutative justice by which the official is charged with the faithful discharge of his duties in the public employ.

The reverse of the Commandment's coin, of course, is that those who place public officials in power—whether the electorate through their votes, or the appointing official through superior authority —have obligations of their own to see that honest and qualified persons are elected or named to their office or position. It is wrong for a political leader to name to office individuals who are not qualified; **it** is wrong to sell public offices; it is wrong to demand graft in exchange for appointment or favor. On the other hand, it is likewise wrong—in lesser kind, to be sure—for members of the electorate to be indifferent with respect to the process by which their political figures are raised up. Interest is incumbent upon any electorate. At the minimum, this means participating in the elective process. Voting is a right, but not a disdaining right. The individual has the personal responsibility to exercise that right and by this action help see that men and women of integrity and competency are chosen to defend and promote the common good. It may not be a sin to neglect to vote. But people who do not vote must first tax their own consciences for political figures and political situations on which the electorate might justifiably sit in judgment.

All of which is to say that there is in the moral equation of the Modern Catholic a factor falling under the heading "social sin." Social sin is a nebulous thing. It does not receive a separate topic heading or index reference in most Catholic handbooks —not even in the *New Catholic Encyclopedia,* for that matter. But to the Modern Catholic it is as real a sin as the embezzlement of a bank or the theft of someone's automobile, and more serious a sin than, say, most sins of the flesh.

Father Peter Henriot dwells on this sense of social

sin in *Commonweal Paper: 5,* dealing with faith and the struggle to believe. He wrote of his dismay upon picking up an otherwise excellent, up-to-date missal explanation of the Sacrament of Penance, and finding that its examination-of-conscience section focused entirely on individual morality: Missing Mass on the appointed days, disobedience to those in authority, lapses in charity, anger within one's own family, etc. He found there not even a hint that there was such a thing as social sin—no awareness of the possible existence of what he termed "structural injustice and our own involvement in its continuance."

Specifically, what does Father Henriot define as social sin? He does not mention voting, but he is categorical about the following: "Racism in the institutions of American society, economic hardships imposed on the poor in the country and in the Third World because of inequitable business practices, waste of scarce global resources through affluent consumption patterns, dominance of the powerless through political manipulation, the increasing danger of annihilation because of the arms race." These, he noted with indisputable accuracy so far as the Modern Catholic is concerned, are evils just as real in our world "as marital infidelity or dishonesty in speech." These are social sins, and Father Henriot is emphatic that they involve persons in terms of responsibility. "Any morality based on responsibility must take them into account."

Father Henriot proceeds to a conclusion that is impossible to fault, whether one is thinking in the contexts of the Seventh or the Tenth Commandments—or, indeed, any of the other eight Commandments. He writes: "A faith which satisfies itself on the level of personal morality is simply truncated and unreal in today's world. It contributes nothing to a mature person's ability to relate to a world where justice is the major issue in human affairs. Social responsibility—which implies an appreciation of and relationship to the structural and institutional aspects of reality—must be central to an integral faith."

Elements, of course, in the general insensitivity to social sin are, as Father Henriot says, both a lack of understanding of social morality and a failure to perceive the structural complexity of social problems. In his view, the difficulty is basically one of perception. The individual simply does not *see* the reality of structural injustice. Thus, no matter how much the individual may profess his or her moral commitment to better the lot of the poor, unless the individual perceives the operation and impact of certain economic systems which make it possible for the poor (people or nations) to control their own destiny, that individual is merely moralistic and not political

—that is, he or she is not effective in bringing change.

For Catholics, Modern or otherwise, the problem here is real, and, it might appear, much bigger than the ability most of us possess as individuals for effectively coping with the challenges presented. Still, much can be done. The individual can make a constant, conscientious effort to be aware of the lot of the socially disenfranchised, and can apply to problem situations such social remedies as the teaching Church provides. (Catholic social doctrine is still a neglected value.) Likewise, the teaching Church, from pope to preacher in the pulpit, must never be hesitant about challenging mindsets, racial and cultural biases, ignorance and intellectual sloth, or whatever else may put religious and social instincts out of touch with human needs of the wider world. This is not an easy task, and, for those in the pulpit and in leadership posts, not a particularly popular one either. It is always so much less trouble to be abstract and morally detached. Yet in a world where the horizons narrow perceptibly each day, and where a social act in one place may have implications anywhere else in the world, no other course is morally defensible than one that tests and criticizes givens in order to better the common good of all humanity.

A concomitant of all of this, in the United States

as elsewhere, is the right that the working person has to employment, to a just wage, to protection from unnecessary hazards in labor conditions, to reasonable security in his or her employment, to the means to support self and family in decent comfort. In effect, this translates to ability to be able to afford living space, food, education, adequate medical care and at least occasional relaxation from the cares and pressures of everyday life. (Is it fair that recreation should be so totally pegged to means?)

One danger related to the Tenth Commandment —"You shall not covet your neighbor's house," or, as I prefer, *goods*—is the possible exaltation of goods, or property, as the supreme consideration in human relationships. It is a danger especially apparent in this civilization of the West, ours, that allegedly lives by the Ten Commandments, or some identifiable ethical variant thereof.

Private property and the rights of ownership are basic concepts in the Catholic Church's (and capitalism's) idea of the just social order. That the concepts have been abused, twisted, misinterpreted, misunderstood, overly inflated with significance goes almost without saying. We all have our choice examples. My thoughts inevitably leap to the time an editor of *America,* the Jesuit weekly, editorialized on the right of an owner of a bomb shelter to protect

83

that property from panicky neighbors in the instance of crisis (enemy attack) by the use of gunfire against the neighbors. (Friend, stay away from my door.) There are numerous other examples. The United States government, for one, has often demonstrated, via the crushing of heads and the bloodying of noses (if not worse), that property is a value of frequently overriding consideration. We all know cases of corporate buildings and institutions being protected against demonstrating people. The same is not always true in reverse. The American corporation is too often free to exploit people at will, particularly those a continent away.

Abuse of the Tenth Commandment thus comes in the virtual divinization of its negative admonition: "You shall not covet your neighbor's house," or property. The admonition sometimes seems to make ownership, by indirection, sacrosanct. So, too, property and goods. What becomes obscured is that ownership is not an absolute right; nor is the status quo always to be held sacred. Pope John XXIII made this plain in incorporating some words of Pius XII into his social encyclical, *Mater et Magistra:* "In defending the right of private property, the Church has in mind a very important ethical aim in social matters. She does not, of course, strive to uphold the present state of affairs as if it were an expression of the divine will. And even less does she accept the patronage of the affluent and wealthy, while neglecting the rights of the poor and the needy. . . . The Church rather does intend that the institution of private property be such as is required by the plan of divine wisdom and the law of nature" (111). In modern times, the Church has regularly restated this precept against economic liberalism, Marxist collectivism, and, to an extent, capitalism itself. Accompanying insistences on the right of labor to organize, on fair wages, on safe and healthy working conditions, on adequate housing have also aimed at driving home the principle that ownership is not without its attendant responsibilities, that it is not to be indulged as one pleases. Nevertheless, a considerable gap exists between ecclesiastical principle and the secular reality —not merely in Communist countries, where the state has assumed complete ownership of property and goods (not always with disastrous results, be it admitted), but more particularly in supposedly enlightened democratic countries of conscience (or concern, at least) such as our own. The American multi-national corporation is, by-and-large, one of the scandals of the Twentieth Century.

The sense of the Tenth Commandment, quite simply, is that ownership is not an unqualified thing —freedom to do as one wills, when and where one wills. Nor is property an end in itself. For just as the acquisitive instinct cannot be free of moral restraints, neither, to repeat, can ownership be free of social responsibilities to people as a whole—as distinct, for instance, from responsibilities to stock holders solely or primarily. This is true not only in terms of the production of goods and services, in the rewarding of workers for work done, of people for land used or taken, or whatever. It is true, too, in terms of vested wealth and invested capital. There is a responsibility that these funds serve other than the selfish, personal ends of the possessor. In this context, philanthropy becomes a good and important expression of one's responsibility to and concern for the rest of humanity. But the Modern Catholic is unconvinced that philanthropy always satisfies the prerequisites of social justice. Nelson Rockefeller's largesse, for instance, is impressive. But in the light of revelations connected with his Vice Presidential nomination, it must be wondered whether the claims of social justice would not have been much better fulfilled if that largesse had been bestowed more on the truly needy than on already affluent executives of Rockefeller projects and on Rockefeller foundations and interests of uncompelling importance. By the kindest interpretation, this is questionable philanthropy. As the Vice Presidential proceedings bore out, much of the Rockefeller philanthropy reflected credit neither on giver nor receiver.

How much more inspiring, and responsible, was

the example of Mother Teresa of Calcutta, the famed Sister of the poor and the dying. She revealed recently that she once refused a check for $500,000, because it was intended as a "security" fund for her missionaries, as distinct from a fund to finance her work among those destitute and forlorn. Here is a lesson not to be missed: Social responsibility is more than the mere giving of anything—and more than the reflexive acceptance of what is offered. The purpose to which the largesse is directed, as well as the need being met, are ultimately what count most.

Chapter Eight

EIGHTH COMMANDMENT

You shall not bear false witness against your neighbor
(Ex. 20:16).

In seeking to fix the place of false witness on the comparative scale of malices, Thomas Aquinas located detraction as a malice less than homicide or adultery, but greater than theft. His reasoning was that, of all external possessions, a person's good name is the most valuable, and therefore not to be lightly toyed with. It is a reasoning solidly rooted in the Old Testament; "A good name is more precious than great riches," says Proverbs, 22:1. And it is a feeling reflected constantly in life and in literature. An anguished Cassio dramatizes the meaning of a good name while reflecting on its loss in Shakespeare's *Othello:* "Reputation, reputation, reputation! Oh! I have lost my reputation. I have lost the immortal part of myself, and what remains is bestial. My reputation, Iago, my reputation!"

The thrust of the Eighth Commandment is to protect good names by insisting on truth as a reflex in the decent person. Transgressions of the Commandment are sins of the tongue, mind and heart, and fall under several topic headings. The principal ones are handled in the succeeding pages:

Defamation is the disparagement or blackening of another's name or reputation. The *New Catholic Encyclopedia* identifies two sinful extremes of defamatory action: The unadorned lie and unreserved truthfulness. A lie is a lie, and hardly needs explication; unreserved truthfulness involves the revelation, without need or necessity, of protected "blackening truths." Defamation is more than uncharitable speech; it is an act of injustice.

Detraction is the extreme of defamation involving unreserved truthfulness. It is an act whereby a person willfully demeans the reputation or worth of another with a view towards lessening him or her in the esteem of others. The motive might be envy; it might be sheer malice. Whatever it is, detraction is a wrong, and like other sins against the Eighth Commandment, the wrong demands reparation—just as surely as does stealing or wrongful damage to another's property. The trouble, of course, is that the harm done by detraction is seldom, if ever, completely undone.

Unreserved truthfulness allows of certain exceptions, as when the rights of the person about whom something discreditable is known conflict with the rights of another, or others, or the common good.

John Dean, for instance, hardly seems to have been guilty of detraction in his unreserved truthfulness about Richard Nixon. However, a person would indeed be guilty of detraction who divulged the background, say, of individuals who, having satisfied the past, have changed identities, moved to another section of the country, and there live as respectable citizens (e.g., informants in criminal court cases).

Calumny, the other extreme of defamation, is the deliberate injury to a person's name or reputation through a direct lie. Calumny is sometimes called slander, but whatever its name, it is one of the most reprehensible of Eighth Commandment transgressions. Again, this is a sin against justice, and must be repaired. Sometimes this repair may involve a monetary settlement—although, it should be pointed out, money never satisfies completely the obligation to right a wrong. The calumniator must also withdraw the false statements and seek, as best can, to restore the name and reputation blackened, even though this may mean the tarnishing of his or her own reputation.

Talebearing is usually a lesser transgression of the Eighth Commandment. In the *New Catholic Encyclopedia* definition, talebearing is the telling of "unfavorable things" that blacken names and, in the process, cause unnecessary harm or sorrow to another. The "unfavorable" item may in fact be truth itself, but that does not mean restraints are off. The possessor of unfavorable knowledge about another is still bound by a responsible tact and by charity. So true is this that talebearing is licit only when there is a moral demand of equal or greater urgency for revelation of the information, as when the continued ignorance of a certain truth may be causing, or threatening, harm.

Gossip is generally light conversation involving confidences, secrets or just plain rumors about another, usually acquaintances, relatives or neighbors. Though the conversation may be "light," the gravity of the involvement is not also necessarily light. Gossip can be an offense against the virtue of fidelity (as when secrets are divulged); it may border on detraction and calumny. Nor does the truth of a set of facts excuse gossip; gossip involving truth can be a sin against charity.

Falsity, which is not to be confused with statement made through ignorance, is the opposite of truth and an evil of the intellect, depriving it, as theologians say, of the good for which it is intended. For purposes of our consideration, a falsity is simply —or purely—a lie; a lie is a statement at variance with the mind of the speaker. To lie is intrinsically wrong because it is opposed to man's rational and social nature, and can therefore never be justified. There are, of course, jocose lies (those told in jest) and "white" lies (those characterized by innocence or minor intent). Neither is often very serious. A malicious lie is something else again, in that it involves intent to injure, to mislead, to hurt. It is inexcusable, and serious to the extent of the harm done.

Under falsity, one encounters *equivocation*, or the use of words or expressions susceptible to two or more meanings, and designed to convey a misleading or wrong impression; and one encounters *mental reservation*, or the introduction of a tacit limitation into a statement or act when it is considered inconvenient or awkward to speak openly. Each is a form of duplicity, though either may on occasion be permissible, as when necessary to preserve a legitimate secret.

Perjury, in essence, is a false statement supported by an oath to which God is invoked as witness. As such, it is considered a sin against the Second Commandment forbidding the taking of the name of God in vain, and is discussed briefly in the chapter dealing with that Commandment. But perjury may also be considered a sin against the Eighth Commandment in that it likewise involves lying. In sum, perjury constitutes a serious offense which, in the opinion of moralists, can only be mitigated by imperfection in the act—insufficient reflection, for instance.

An oath is not something to be regarded casually

by the swearer, nor, for that matter, something to be frivolously administered. An official who administers an oath to one known to be swearing falsely is as guilty of wrongdoing in the one direction as the false swearer is in the other.

At the same time, oaths should not be multiplied, nor trivialized. They should be reserved for serious occasions and responsible duties. Thus it seems reasonable to expect a new mayor or a new congressman to swear an oath of fidelity upon taking office. The same would not appear to be so for one assuming the post of dog-catcher or village recreation commissioner (the examples are not so preposterous as they might sound). Nor would oaths seem a necessary prerequisite, as has been the case, for students in order to qualify for a loan from a public agency. To require oaths willy-nilly is both to increase unnecessarily the grounds for possible perjury and to reduce the significance of oaths themselves. No one wants to see the swearing of oaths reduced to the meaninglessness of the "Star Spangled Banner." But just as the "Star Spangled Banner" has been demeaned by ritualistic use in public event upon public event (e.g., sporting contests almost without exception), so are oaths discounted, their significance neutralized, by overuse.

Before leaving perjury, one word: Sycophants who lend willing ears to lies and detractions, to statements that cause injury and dissension, are not excused from culpability in the wrong committed. In other words, one must be pure of ear as of tongue.

In contradistinction to Thomas Aquinas' gauging degrees of malice, it would be presumptuous to suggest that one Commandment more than another is held in particular esteem by the Modern Catholic. Yet in any hierarchical arrangement of the Commandments (an arrangement that would certainly be led by the Fifth), the Eighth would surely rank high, since it deals with truth and with honesty— both scarred virtues, but both newly reverenced perhaps because having been so badly used by people preaching respect for both. The times have seen a special emphasis placed on love and openness, charity and truth, honesty of thought and of expression— particularly among the young. Consciously or not, the result has been a new sensitivity to what the Eighth Commandment is all about.

In this context, those responding positively to the Commandment's injunctions sense that the spirit of the Commandment extends to groups and to classes just as surely as it does to individuals. Specifically, they are sensitive to the fact that the Eighth discourages the malicious characterization of a people (as of Boston blacks by the South Boston Irish) or body (as of the Democrat Senators running in the 1972 election by then-President Nixon: "They're, they're crooks, they've been stealing, they've been taking . . ."). Accountability for such talk may be avoided in law, but it cannot be avoided in conscience merely because the defamation is not directed at an individual, inferentially or by name.

By final word, let it be noted that the Eighth Commandment falls within that classification of "do not" admonitions that are not fully observed unless honored also in the opposite of what is forbidden. The Eighth Commandment reproves contempt, hate, unfairness in thought and in word. Accordingly, it enjoins the person to respect, love, justice and fairness —the core elements of Christianity.